PYTHON LANGUAGE FOR TEENS

By professor U.Hartley

Contents

3

Description

Teenagers who wish to learn Python and are interested in programming should take this course. Additionally, it gives some fundamental knowledge of Python, which is useful for studying the language further. It has basic exercises, quizzes, and examples that may help you learn Python.

To make sense of enormous datasets, Python is a computer language that has grown in popularity in the data science sector. With sufficient practise, the language is simple to pick up and may be learned quickly. It is ideal for novices because of its simple syntax and readability. Python's versatility makes it useful for a wide range of tasks, including web applications, software development, scripting, data analysis, machine learning, and artificial intelligence. Not just major corporations, but also startups looking for a less expensive option to expensive coding services, are in need of Python developers. Additionally, I have a professional describing Python's abilities and how they relate to AI (AI)

Describe programming.

Programming, to put it as simply as possible, is the process of creating code that tells a computer how to carry out a job.

A job might be as simple as multiplying two integers or as challenging as launching a spacecraft into orbit!

A statement, or single command to the computer, is the smallest component of a programme.

After you've finished writing your programme, a compiler turns your code into machine code, the computer's most basic language. The central processing unit, or CPU, receives instructions from machine code on how to accomplish tasks like loading a value or completing some math.

When someone says, "I compiled my software," they indicate that they changed their source code into machine code.

Why not simply write machine code straight away? The apparent explanation is that computer code is accessible by humans. Below, you may compare a program's Python version with the matching machine code:

Python Programming

"Hello, World!" should be printed.

Equivalent Machine Code

C7: 3c 2a: 3c 2a: 2b: 2a: 5c 3c: 28: 5c 2a: 2b: 2a: 5c 3c: 28: 5c 2a: 2b The following are the numbers: 2a 5c 3c 28 5c 2a 2b 2a 5c 3c 28 5c The following numbers are in order: 2a 2b 2a 5c 3c 28 5c 2a 2b 2a 5c 3c 28 5c 2a 2b 2a 5c 3c 28 5c 2a 2b 2a 5c 3c 28 5c 2a 2b 2a 00 00 01 00 00 00 00 00 00 00 00 00 00 00 00 00 00 64 48 65 6c 6c 6f 2c 20 57 6f 72 6c 64 21 00 00 00 00 00 00 00 00 00 00 00 \s00 00 00 00 00 00 00 00 00 00 00 00 00 00 00 00 \s00 00 00 00 00 00 00 00 00 00 00 00 00 00 00 00 00

...
"Good day, world!"

It is clear why you shouldn't directly write in machine code. There are a few individuals that do, however, and taste is subjective:]

There is a little detail that we omitted before. As we hinted at above, Python is an interpreted language; it is not immediately compiled into machine code.

Python instead makes use of a tool called an Interpreter. Another software that converts code into Bytecode, which is subsequently translated into machine code while the programme is executed, is an interpreter. After here, you'll read more about interpreters.

When the programme is ultimately launched, the newly compiled machine code is put into memory and read by the CPU to carry out the programme.

To begin programming with Python, you don't really need to understand how compilers function, but you need first make sure that Python is installed.

The Beginning

Python is preloaded on a Mac, which is great news if you're using one.

Open Terminal.app to access the Python interpreter on a Mac. You may do this by searching for it in Spotlight or by looking in your Applications/Utilities folder.

Open Terminal, then enter and press the following command.

Python is priced at $.

What you should see should resemble what follows:

Python 2.76 (v2.7.6:3a1db0d2747e, Nov 10 2013, 00:42:54) (dot) [GCC 4.2.1 (Apple Inc. build 5666)] to darwin

To learn more, use "help", "copyright", "credits," or "licence"

The output from Terminal should be posted in the topic if you don't achieve the results shown above, and we'll do our best to assist you.

Windows

On Windows, the procedure is little more complicated, but then again, Windows is where most things are! :]

Go to the Python downloads page on the official website first.

Python software is available for download at www.python.org/download.

Go to opensource.com/life/14/3/goog to read @opensourceway's blog article about @soc and @sopw.

Expand Python Software @ThePOF and both use Python.

5 Mar

For our paid internships via the GNOME Outreach Program for Women, there are just two weeks left to apply.

Python Software Expansion @ThePOF

3 Mar

PyLadies: promoting CPython summer internships that are compensated googl/W04

Include more Python software @ThePSF

27 Feb

Python in the 2014 Google Summer of Code goo.gl/760H4

Python software expansion @ThePSE

Send a tweet to @ThePSP 27 Pub.

Python download Python download

Python 2.7.6 and Python 3.4.0 are the current production versions.

If you want the maximum stability or to learn Python, start with one of these versions; they are both regarded as reliable production releases.

Python 3.4 should be used if you are unsure about which version to use. If you need to utilise any current third-party software that is not yet Python 3 compatible, you should download Python 2.7.x.

Check out the comprehensive Python 3.4.0 page for the MD5 Checksums and OpenPGP signatures:

• MSI Installer for Windows x86 for Python 3.4.0 (Windows binary does not include source)

• Python 3.4.0 Windows X86-64 MSI Installer (Windows AMD64/Intel 64/X86-64 binaries [1]; excludes source code)

• Mac OS X 64-bit/32-bit x86-64/1386 Installer for Python 3.4.0 (for Mac OS X 10.6 and later [2])

• Mac OS X 32-bit 1386/PPC Installer for Python 3.4.0 (for Mac OS X 10.5 and later [2])

• The source tarball for Python 3.4.0. (for Linux, Unix or Mac OS X)

• Source tarball with Python 3.4.0 xzipped (for Linux, Unix or Mac OS X, better compression)

Visit the thorough Python 2.7.6 website to learn more about MD5 Checksums and OpenPGP signatures:

Scroll all the way down to Python 2.7.x after passing the Python 3.x.x versions. Run the Windows installer you downloaded, follow the prompts, and accept the default settings as you go.

You must start the interpreter after the installer is complete.

Launching the interpreter in Windows Vista or Windows 7 is done as follows:

In the bottom left corner, select the Start button.

Select All Programs.

Open the Python folder.

To run the IDLE interpreter twice

Using Windows 8, start the interpreter by doing the following:

In the bottom left corner, choose the Start button.

IDLE in the search field

Select IDLE (Python GUI)

To reach Python 2.7.x, scroll past the Python 3.x.x versions. Run the Windows installer after downloading it, then follow the on-screen directions while accepting the default settings.

You need to run the interpreter after the installer is finished.

Launch the interpreter as follows on Windows Vista or Windows 7:

Start by clicking the icon in the bottom left corner.

Choose "All Programs"

Dispatch the Python folder

the IDLE interpreter by two clicks

Launch the interpreter using these steps if you're using Windows 8:

Start by clicking the icon in the bottom left corner.

In the search bar, enter IDLE.

Click IDLE.

Search \sEverywhere

Python GUI IDLE (Python GUI IDLE)

Blend \sidlebrain \sStudi
\sidlewild \sHyper

idle hands idle air control valve
symptoms idle mach mine idlewild
baptist church

Regardless of how you started the
interpreter, you must ensure that it
functions properly. In Windows'
Command Prompt or the Terminal,
enter the following command:

scribble "Hello World!"

You've just finished writing your
first Python program, despite the
fact that it doesn't seem like much.
Printing The default greeting when

learning the majority of languages is frequently "Hello, World."

Instead of printing it to your printer, the print command instructs the computer to print the next few lines on the screen! Observe the quotation marks around "Hello World"; anything inside them is treated as regular text and won't be taken to mean an instruction.

Variables

As you program, you'll use variables A LOT as a way to store data in the computer's memory. Variables may have a specific type in some languages that designates the class to which they belong.

Your variable types do not need to be declared in Python. This information will be covered in more detail a little later in the tutorial, so don't worry about it too much right now.

Press Enter after entering the following command into the interpreter:

hello equals "Hello World!"

This declares the variable "hello" and sets its value to "Hello World." Now you can use the hello variable instead of manually entering "Hello World" wherever it is needed in your program.

Press Enter after entering the following command into the interpreter:

type "hi"

The output of this is identical to that of your Hello World example, but it prints the value of the hello variable.

Numbers can be stored in variables as well. The following commands should be entered into your interpreter:

```
x = 5 print x y = 10 print z z = x + y
print
```

Types of Variable

Earlier in this course, you came across variable types, but we didn't go into great depth about them. Different types of values are stored by various variable types.

A comprehensive list of Python's built-in types may be found in the language's official documentation.

Strings and integers are the only two fundamental kinds you have worked with in Python so far. Additionally, boolean types will be present, which you may use to hold True and False values.

Here is some further information on each of these variable types:

Integers

Whole numbers are known as integers. On 32-bit devices, integers vary between -2147483648 and 2147483647, and on 64-bit machines, between -9223372036854775808 and 9223372036854775807

As seen below, you may construct an integer variable by just inputting the number without any quotation marks:

foo = 5

Strings

A string is a group of characters that may be used to represent anything, including text on a screen and whole web requests.

As seen below, you create a string variable by enclosing the string of characters in quotation marks:

bar is "foo-bar."

Booleans

Boolean values are either True or False.

As seen below, you may construct a boolean variable simply putting True or False in capital letters without using quotation marks.

'sFoo' = 'True'

The variable is not surrounded by quotation marks; if it were, you would be defining True as a string variable rather than a variable!

Python Concatenation of String and Int

Example

Let's have a look at an example of how the + operator may be used to combine a string (str) with an integer (int).

Year is, string concat int.py current year message =

year current = 2018

current year message plus current year is printed.

The string: is what we want to come out. 2018 is the year. However, the following runtime error occurs when we execute this code:

Traceback (last call is the most recent):

String concat int.py, line 5, in module>, file "/Users/sammy/Documents/github/journaldev/Python-3/basic examples/strings"

current year message plus current year is printed.

Can only concatenate str (not "int") to str due to a type error

In Python, how do you concatenate str and int? There are numerous additional approaches to carry out this action.

Prerequisites
You will require the following to complete this tutorial:

knowledge of installing Python 3. and proficiency with Python programming. Using VS Code for Python or the Python 3 series of tutorials.

Python 3.9.6 was used to test this tutorial.

str() Function usage

The str() function accepts an int argument and converts it to a str:

str(current year) + print(current year message)

The string "Year is 2018" is returned for the current year integer.

With printf-style String Formatting, we can pass values to a conversion specification when using the% Interpolation Operator:

(current year message, current year) print("%s%s"

The string "Year is 2018" is interpolated from the current year integer:

Using the str.format() function We can also concatenate a string and an integer using the str.format() function.

format(current year message, current year) print("".

A string is created by type-coercing the current year integer: 2018 is the year.

f-string use

You can use f-strings if you are running Python 3.6 or a later version.

print(f'{current year message}{current year}')

A string is interpolated from the current year integer: 2018 is the year.

Python Simplified for Teens

Therefore, your adolescent is considering acoding. It's never too early to start learning, but with so many possibilities available, where should one start? Many would claim that Python, a well-known text-based programming language, provides the solution to that question. To help you get started with Python for adolescents, this post will showcase a few of the various online courses, tutorials, and books that are available.

Python exploration for kids in middle and high school

It's a terrific time for kids in middle and high schools to begin programming. Let's get started with Python programming to learn how to code for adolescents.

In the world of programming, Python is one of the most popular languages. In fact, according to recent surveys, it ranks third among all languages worldwide. This wide-spread acceptance of Python is attributable to a number of elements, such as its straightforward syntax, sizeable library, and usage in a number of different applications, all of which contribute to the language's suitability as a learning tool. Python is an excellent programming language to learn for practical applications as well, since it is used by many well-known corporations, such as Google, Facebook, and Instagram.

Online live, coached sessions are among the finest methods to learn

Python. In this environment, students have access to knowledgeable instructors who can respond to their questions as they arise throughout the course of learning. In guided courses, the curriculum is planned and the material is arranged in a way that reduces confusion and is well-paced.

Trinket.io Instructions

Python-specific Hour of Code lessons are available for free on Trinket.io for students who prefer a hands-on, independent learning style. Through the use of Python turtle visuals, this crash course covers loops, conditional statements, functions, and objects.

Free Python Course on Udemy

Python courses on Udemy are of the same high calibre as those in other programming languages. People with no previous Python or programming expertise should take this course. More than an hour and a half of free lecture videos are available for this course, and they provide a great place to start for a beginner programmer.

Teenage Python courses that are the best

Teenagers that like autonomous work and instructor contact will do well in Python classes. In order to ensure that the skills students acquire are relevant to the real world, they also have curriculums that were created by specialists in the area of technology.

The Python for AI course offered by Create & Learn, created by specialists from Google, Stanford, and MIT, is a fantastic illustration of this. There are four units in this course, each having four lessons of 70 minutes. Students must complete a new game or assignment in each lesson, with the difficulty of each one increasing over time. Additionally, students have additional assignments they may work on outside of class to put the concepts they learned into practise.

Some of the greatest schools also help students develop new abilities gradually, reducing frustration by subtly introducing new ideas. For instance, using our learning paths, students will be prepared to start studying Pandas Data Science after they have finished Python for AI. Pandas + Python is a potent combo that will aid in your child's exploration of an engaging area and help them comprehend the basics of data science.

Students may get free Python courses and exercises.

After learning the fundamentals of Python, students may hone their abilities with activities like these!

1. Construct a simple Python chatbot

This chatbot exercise is a wonderful way to learn about loops, I/O, and text manipulation in Python, as well as the "random" package. Additionally, students may get creative with how their chatbot responds to user input!

2. Tutorial for Python Lists

One of the first data structures that Python novices must understand is the list. The idea is rather straightforward and lays the groundwork for future more complex data structures.

3. For Loops Basics

Given that they are utilised in almost every programme, for loops are a crucial subject to comprehend in programming. This is a wonderful lesson since it provides examples for students to utilise in a range of situations, including lists, strings, and more.

4. Test out Pandas for data science

It could be beneficial for students who have been using Python for a few weeks to play with the "pandas" package. Data science for data analytics uses a programme called Pandas, which is short for "panel data." Although it has real-world professional applications, students can most definitely study it as well. To see whether your kid might be interested in this area of computer science, read this introduction!

games for beginners in Python

A wonderful method to learn how to code is to make games. Students' conditional reasoning abilities are tested using games that ask what circumstance causes a player to win or lose. Additionally, it makes students consider how users will interact with their work. What happens, for instance, if a player enters letters rather than numbers into a game? Learning how to build a game in Python to create the Hogwarts sorting hat might be a nice introduction for people who have never done so before. The 21 Game, which is simply a guessing game played against a computer, is another game to try designing.

Books on Python for adolescents

Here are some Python books for teenagers to check out if they study better with additional instruction or prefer reading to pick up new abilities.

Python for Teens 1.

This book teaches students the fundamentals of Python in addition to white-hat hacking, web design, and debugging. Students may choose which area of computer science they would wish to go further by using Python to study these many topic areas.

Python Programming for Students 2.

This book is a helpful tool for those who want to approach Python with a more mathematical mindset. Instead of syntax, it emphasises problem-solving and algorithms. This book, which is beneficial to students generally pursuing STEM careers, includes important chapters on trigonometric functions and charting.

3. Python Programming for the Arts, Games, and More: 30+ Projects

Instead of providing students with straightforward teaching material, Creative Coding in Python adopts a different strategy by giving them a broad choice of tasks to try out. The chances this book offers for creation will appeal to those who are interested in art or game design.

Teenagers should learn Python.
That's a lot to process, my goodness! To wrap up, here is a brief summary:

Python, one of the most widely used programming languages worldwide, is often used to introduce beginners to programming.

Instructor-led classes provide a methodical approach to learning Python that may help you gain confidence and guarantee that you advance quickly.

Independent learners can like working via tutorials and exercises in addition to lessons.

If you're still unsure about where to start, the acclaimed free Intro to Python AI course from Create & Learn is a well-liked option. Happy coding!